Jane Yolen

The Library of Author Biographies

Jane Yolen

Susanna Daniel

The Rosen Publishing Group, Inc., New York

For Curtis

Published in 2004 by The Rosen Publishing Group, Inc.
29 East 21st Street, New York, NY 10010

Library of Congress Cataloging-in-Publication Data
Daniel, Susanna.
Jane Yolen / Susanna Daniel.— 1st ed.
    p. cm. — (The library of author biographies)
Summary: A biography of Jane Yolen, a prolific and well-known writer of juvenile literature.
Includes bibliographical references and index.
ISBN 0-8239-4015-2 (lib. bdg.)
1. Yolen, Jane. 2. Authors, American—20th century—Biography. 3. Children's literature—Authorship. [1. Yolen, Jane. 2. Authors, American. 3. Women—Biography.] I. Title.
II. Series.
PS3575.O43 Z64 2003
813'.54—dc21

                                                    2002154270

Manufactured in the United States of America

Table of Contents

Introduction:
A Writer's
Adventures

In the attic of her fourteen-room farmhouse in Hatfield, Massachusetts—a tiny town with a population of only 3,000 people— Jane Yolen keeps two monstrous desks piled high with books, papers, photographs, and other assorted and valuable clutter. At one desk, Yolen writes poems, fairy tales, folktales, short stories, and novels. At the other desk, she reads other people's writing and gives them feedback. Yolen starts writing early in the morning and continues through to the late afternoon. She writes every single day, except holidays.

7

Jane Yolen has been a writer since she first learned how to write. She wrote poems before she even started school. In second grade, she wrote the music and lyrics for her class play about vegetables, in which she played the lead carrot. For the finale, the whole cast jumbled together to make a big salad.

Contrary to how Yolen's life might appear now—peaceful and organized—she has had many adventures. When she was a teenager, she took ballet lessons from a famous ballerina named Maria Tallchief. In her twenties, she hiked up Mount Pelion in Greece while seven and a half months pregnant with her first child, Heidi. She also worked on a kibbutz (a communal farm) in Israel, drove a dog sled in Alaska, and snorkeled in the Red Sea—the body of water that separates northeastern Africa from western Asia. Once, she chased her father into Long Island Sound, in New York, where he was dragged on a windy day by a twelve-foot-by-twelve-foot kite. (Yolen's dad was an international kite flying champion.)

Also, she gave birth to three kids, who in turn had three kids each, so she's a grandmother nine times over. Perhaps her most impressive achievement is that she sold her first book on her twenty-second birthday. To date, Jane Yolen has published more than 230 books.

An Ancient Tradition

Because she mostly writes stories that are folktales or fairy tales, Jane Yolen has been called "the Hans Christian Andersen of America"[1] by *Newsweek* and "a modern equivalent of Aesop"[2] by the *New York Times*. It might seem strange for people to compare Yolen to these classic storytellers. After all, Hans Christian Andersen, who was Danish, lived from 1805 to 1875 and wrote many fairy tales that have since become famous, including "The Ugly Duckling" and "The Emperor's New Clothes." And Aesop lived in ancient Greece, around the year 500 BC. He told stories that involved animals with human characteristics. Aesop's stories are called fables because they contain a warning or moral, which is like a message.

Jane Yolen, who was born about 2,500 years after Aesop and 100 years after Hans Christian Andersen, also writes stories that contain important moral messages. Generally, though, her stories tend to be a little longer than Aesop's and Andersen's, and her messages tend to be a little less obvious. Many of her stories might be considered modern fairy tales or folktales.

Fairy Tales and Folktales

Many fairy tales are also allegories, or stories that use imaginary situations to get across a message or idea. Originally, fairy tales involved magical creatures, like gnomes, elves, brownies, banshees, sylphs, sprites, goblins, pixies, and kobolds. (What's a kobold? It's an invisible household goblin with a friendly nature, found in early German folktales. You can look in the glossary at the back of this book to find out about the other creatures.) Early folktales—which were circulated orally through storytelling instead of written down and published—contained many such creatures. Later, these creatures appeared in classic tales, like the fairies in Shakespeare's play *A Midsummer Night's Dream* (1600) and in *Tales of Mother Goose* (1696). Perhaps the most famous fairy tales are those by the brothers Jacob Ludwig Karl Grimm and Wilhelm Karl Grimm, who collected and published early versions of such tales as "Hansel and Gretel" and "Snow White and the Seven Dwarves."

Where Fairy Tales Meet Fantasy Stories

Jane Yolen's books, which usually involve a large variety of characters—animals and fantastical creatures as well as ordinary humans—are set in a variety of places, including imaginary planets far, far from Earth. Here is a sampling, to give you a sense of some of the different worlds Yolen writes about: Her book *Wizard's Hall* (published in 1991 and preceding the Harry Potter books by eight years) is about a boy wizard who tries hard and never gives up, then ends up saving his entire school. *The Transfigured Hart* (1975) is about a boy, a girl, and an albino deer who, one enchanted night, is transformed into a unicorn. *Sister Light, Sister Dark* (1988), a story of sorcery and prophecy, involves a young girl who is called on to reunite a broken kingdom. *Armageddon Summer* (1998), written with Yolen's friend, writer Bruce Coville, is about a boy and a girl who fall in love while forced by their families to live with a mountaintop cult that is anticipating the end of the world.

Some of Yolen's books—like *Armageddon Summer*—aren't strictly folktales or fairy tales. But it can be said that all of her stories stretch the limits of imagination and attempt to answer the all-important question "What if?" For example, what if, during her family's seder (a ceremonial Jewish meal), a teenage girl went back in time and experienced a concentration camp during the Holocaust? This happens in *The Devil's Arithmetic* (1988). Or, what if two young girls, having been raised by a pack of wolves, were found by humans and placed in an orphanage? This story is told in *Children of the Wolf* (1984).

In addition to these topics, Yolen has written a book about female pirates called *Pirates in Petticoats* (1963); a book about a Chinese emperor and his young daughter, called *The Emperor and the Kite* (1968); and a book about a teenage romance set in a Shaker community in England in the 1850s, called *The Gift of Sarah Barker* (1981).

Where Stories Come From

Some themes tend to turn up more frequently than others in Yolen's books. For instance, the theme of friendship appears in almost all of her middle school and young adult stories, as do the themes of human connection, death and loss, multiculturalism (the joining of many cultures), and family. Yolen has written collections of poems and picture books for children, as well as collections of songs. She's also written novels for adults and nonfiction books, including a guide to her very own craft—writing for children.

Unlike in her books, there are no goblins or wizards in Jane Yolen's true past, and she has never changed physical form or fought dragons or traveled through time. But she has danced the twist in New York City with dozens of garbage men, and she has ridden a great white Lipizzan horse—a breed of horse that descends from royal Austrian horses dating back to 1580—and she has fallen into the 40°F (4°C) rapids of the Colorado River after being knocked by a wave from her raft.

In an autobiographical essay, Yolen once said she saw a Malaysian merman (like a mermaid, but a man) in Greenwich, England. She swears she did. She even took a photo. If ever you stumble on the opportunity to meet Jane Yolen, ask her to show you the photo. Or, after reading about the strange, exciting, unbeliev-able, and mystical happenings in her books, you can just take her word for it.

1 A Writer Is Born

Jane Yolen was born in New York City on February 11, 1939. In the Yolen household, reading and writing were highly valued activities. Jane's father's grandfather had been a Reb, a Jewish storyteller, in his village in the Ukraine. Jane's father, Will Hyatt Yolen, was an author and publicist, and Jane's mother, Isabelle Berlin Yolen, quit her job as a social worker to raise Jane and her younger brother, Steven. She also wrote stories and crossword puzzles in her spare time.

While her parents were excellent role models for a budding writer, Jane's most important early influences were the classic books she read as a child. Some of the first authors she loved were Louisa May Alcott, who wrote *Little Women* (1868), which is about four sisters growing up during the Civil War; E. B. White, who wrote *Charlotte's Web* (1952), about a pig named Wilbur who befriends a spider named Charlotte; and Robert Louis Stevenson, who wrote *Kidnapped* (1885), the story of a young boy who is orphaned and sent to live with an uncle he has never met, and *Treasure Island* (1882), an adventure story involving a band of pirates.

A History of Telling Stories

Young Jane started writing poems before she even went to school, and by the time she started first grade she was a more advanced reader than her classmates. "When I read a semester's reading book overnight," she wrote in an essay, "the teacher had no alternative but to skip me into second grade. I spent the remainder of my elementary school days at PS 93 [Public School], which is now only a parking lot on Ninety-third Street at Columbus Avenue [in New York City]. I walked to and from school with my best friend Diane Sheffield who lived in the apartment across the hall. She was skinny and blonde, and I was plump and dark, but the boys seemed to pull my pigtails as often as hers. We were both tomboys, and we played rough-and-tumble games in the grass and rocks of Central Park.

"At PS 93 the teachers encouraged my reading and writing. I won gold stars and gold stars and more gold stars. I was the gold star star. And I was pretty impossibly full of myself."[1]

When she was eight years old, Jane—already a regular at the local library—came across a two-volume boxed book in her parents' library at home. She thought the book was beautiful. According to Jane, "It was just such a gorgeous book to touch and feel, so I started reading it. It was Thomas Mann's *Joseph in Egypt*. Probably most of it went right over my head, but I remember the touch of it and I read the whole thing. I just couldn't stop reading."[2] Written in 1934, *Joseph in Egypt* was a fictional—or imagined—interpretation of the life of Joseph from the Bible.

Another early inspiration came from folktales and songs. Jane's father played the guitar and sang, and he encouraged Jane to learn old English, Scottish, Irish, and Appalachian love songs and ballads—she did her homework and soon knew more than he did on the subject. Jane also checked out folktales and fairy stories from the library by the dozens. Jane's family joked that there were only three things that did not interest her as a child: cookbooks, sports, and science.

One sport, though, did interest Jane: kite flying. Kite flying—called kiting—was one of her father's passions. He was photographed flying a kite for *Life* magazine, named for kiting in *The Guinness Book of World Records*, and included in *Ripley's Believe It or Not*. Kite flying would find its way into Jane's writing career as well: In her early twenties, Jane ghostwrote *The Young Sportsman's Guide to Kite Flying* (1969) for her father. (A ghostwriter writes a book without being named as its author. This book is now out of print, meaning that the publisher no longer distributes the book.) Later, kite flying emerged as a theme in Jane's books for kids, *The Emperor and the Kite* (1968) and *World on a String: The Story of Kites* (1968).

Ready, Set, Go . . .
To Middle School

In sixth grade, Jane was accepted at Hunter, a school for gifted students. About this period in her life, Jane wrote, "With my gold stars and my writing ability, I expected to be a superior gift to Hunter. To my surprise—and horror—I was barely in the middle of the class and managed to stay there only by studying extremely hard . . ."[3] She continued:

> Since it was clear that I was not nearly as smart as I had thought, I turned my attention to those gifts I did have. Music became a mainstay in my life. I starred as Hansel in our class [performance] of Humperdinck's *Hansel and Gretel*, though I was about a head shorter than the girl who played Gretel. She had a pure lyric soprano voice, while I had a low alto. I also played a little piano, with more vigor than talent, and liked to write little songs. I also was one of the leading dancers in my class at Balanchine American School of Ballet . . . (In my sixtieth year I would call on my old ballet experience to write a picture book about the *Firebird* ballet.) My writing continued to bring me approval, though Hunter did not give gold stars. I wrote my eighth-grade social studies essay in rhyme. It was all about New York State's manufacturing, with a great rhyme for Otis Elevators, which I have thankfully forgotten. I also wrote my first two books: a nonfiction book on pirates, which I bound with a linen-over-cardboard cover, and a novel. The novel was seventeen pages long and included a trip by

covered wagon across the West, death by snakebite, a plague of locusts, the birth of an infant on the road, a prairie fire, slaughter by Indians, and marriage to a [school teacher]. It was a masterpiece of [brief writing] . . .

This reflected later in my appreciation for the short form. Short stories and poetry have remained my first loves. I have come to writing full-scale novels almost reluctantly, and it is always a struggle for me to make them long enough. Somehow, seventeen pages still seems about right! Music, too, has remained an important part of my writing. Many of my books have been inspired by songs: *Dream Weaver* by a bad rock song; *Bird of Time* by a rock song misheard; *Greyling* and "The White Seal Maid" by a folk song; the solution of "Princess Heart O' Stone" by an Irish ditty.[4]

Jane has also included original song lyrics in many of her books and has written two musical plays and half an opera. She's written songs and song lyrics for folk singers, rock musicians, and composers—some of these have even been recorded. Several of her stories—including *The Magic Three of Solatia* (1974, out of print) and *The Minstrel and the Mountain* (1967, out of print)—are about musicians.

Camp, Religion, and Friends

When she was twelve and thirteen years old, Jane went off to summer camp. "It was a wonderful Quaker camp in Vermont called Indianbrook (now Farm & Wilderness), where [she] learned about pacifism, swimming, storytelling, mucking out [cleaning] horse stalls, planting a garden, and kissing, not necessarily in that order."[5] Quakerism is a sect of Christianity that emphasizes human goodness and personal divinity, or godliness, and stresses peace and opposes war. It was founded in England in the seventeenth century by an activist named George Fox.

At the end of her second summer at camp, her parents—quite unexpectedly—moved the family to Westport, Connecticut, without even giving her an opportunity to return to New York to say good-bye to friends. In Connecticut, Jane attended Bedford Junior High and Staples High School, where she was involved in singing and literary groups, and was captain of the girls' basketball team. She took piano lessons, ballet lessons, and horseback riding lessons, and she won a Scholastic Writing Award for a poem entitled "Death, You Do Not Frighten Me."

At Staples High, Jane became best friends with a girl named Stella Colandrea. Jane and Stella shared a passion for singing and humor (they even coauthored naughty limericks about the boys in their classes), and Stella's Catholic upbringing became an important influence in Jane's work.

Jane was interested in Judaism and Quakerism. However, she was also attracted to Catholic rituals and traditions, which stimulated her imagination and influenced the elaborate religious rituals she later wrote into her fantasy tales.

Another important influence in Jane's high school experience was her cousin Honey Knopp. Honey was a pacifist (a person who opposes war) and a peace activist who hosted small musical parties—called hootenannies at the time—in the home she shared with her husband, Burt. At these gatherings, Jane learned more about the cadences, or tempos and rhythms, of folk music. Honey encouraged Jane's interest in Quakerism. Years later, Jane wrote a biography called *Friend: The Story of George Fox and the Quakers* (1972). The biography, which was written for young, adults, tells of the foundations and history of the Quaker religion.

About her high school years, Jane wrote, "[My] secret, alien, meditative, poetic side I kept well hidden throughout much of high school except from Honey and some of the people I met at her house. This was in the mid-1950s, when to be interested in such things branded one an outsider, a beatnik . . . I adored Honey and her husband, Burt, and their home became my haven. Oh, I still went to basketball games and dances and parties, wisecracking with my friends and being outrageous. But Honey called out another side of me."[6] Honey's calming influence on Jane can be seen in many works, including *The Transfigured Hart* (1975) and *The Gift of Sarah Barker* (1981).

Off to College

After graduating from Staples High, Yolen enrolled at Smith College, an all-women's college in Massachusetts. It was a choice that would change her life by teaching her the value of creating and keeping friendships with women; by introducing her to the New England countryside, which would turn out to be a lifelong love; and by teaching her about poetry and literature.

About her choice to attend Smith, Yolen says, "Smith had not been my first choice. I had wanted to go to Radcliffe (partially because a boyfriend was in Boston) or to Swarthmore, a coed Quaker school. But though I was accepted at Smith, Wellesley, and Oberlin, my two top choices did not want me. I had been high—but not top—of my class, ranked seventh in a class of over two hundred. I had good grades—but not spectacular—test scores. I had been captain of the basketball team, news editor of the paper, head of the Jewish Youth Group, vice president of the Spanish, Latin, and jazz clubs, in the top singing group, winner of the 'I Speak for Democracy' contest, winner of the school's English prize, and contributor to the literary magazine. But still I did not stand out enough. So I chose Smith because Smith emphasized that everyone at Smith sang. I loved singing."[7]

As it turned out, Yolen sang for only a year in the choirs at Smith. She was busy, though, writing poetry, studying English and Russian literature and religion, and taking a variety of classes in history, sociology, and geology. She also discovered that she had a talent for politics and poetry, as well as a gift for performing music on stage. She ran many campus organizations, wrote and performed in class musicals, and wrote a final exam on American intellectual history completely in verse (and earned an A on the paper, despite her lack of understanding of the subject).

But it was poetry and folk singing that became Yolen's main, constant pursuits. Her poetry was published in Smith's *Grecourt Review*, *Poetry Digest*, and other small magazines, and she won every single prize given out for poetry her senior year in college. The folk songs she'd first learned at Honey's home influenced her stories and inspired her interest in oral storytelling.

In high school and college, Yolen held a variety of jobs, including work as a page at the local library, as a camp counselor, as an intern for *Newsweek*, as a volunteer at a Quaker work camp in Ohio, and as a cub reporter for the *Bridgeport Sunday Herald*. (Her first byline—the line beneath the headline in a newspaper that gives the reporter's name—misspelled her name as Joan Yolen. She decided not to take it as a sign that she wasn't meant to continue reporting.)

After graduating from college in 1960, Yolen moved to New York City to start her life as a writer. To make ends meet, she worked first at *This Week* magazine, then at the *Saturday Review*, where she helped lay out the magazine. Yolen was fired from the *Saturday Review* because of personality differences with the production manager, and she spent the next several months working as a freelance writer.

This was when she ghostwrote *The Young Sportsman's Guide to Kite Flying* for her father, and with the help of a friend of the family, wrote short biographical sketches for the *Celebrity Register*.

However, being a freelancer is often very challenging. You have to devote a lot of energy and time to looking for work, and sometimes the pay isn't very good. Yolen found freelancing difficult but ultimately rewarding. As busy and full as her life had been before and during college—with her active social calendar, many clubs and organizations, and academics—it was about to become even more fulfilling.

2 Real Life Begins After College

Two major, life-changing events happened to Jane Yolen during the year after she graduated from Smith College. The first thing that took place was that Yolen was contacted by an editor at Knopf, a publishing house in New York City. The editor had been given Yolen's name by one of her professors at Smith. The editor asked Yolen if she had any full-length book manuscripts, and Yolen, after considering her options, told the editor that she had several books. The editor asked for a meeting.

The trouble was, Yolen had lied about her work. She didn't have any books at all, only a drawer full of partially finished poems. She didn't know what to do, so she sat down at her typewriter and tried to think of the shortest, easiest kind of book to write. Eventually, she had an idea: books for kids. Children's books, Yolen thought, were short and simple; they had to be a cinch to write.

Soon, though, Yolen would learn that children's books are just as difficult to write as books for adults, because although there are fewer words, each word is extremely important.

"I knew very little about children's books," wrote Yolen in an article. "I had been reading adult books since ninth grade . . . What I remembered was—pictures."[1] Pictures, Yolen figured, would take up most of the space on each page of a children's book. But there was still one huge problem: She couldn't draw. Fortunately, an old high school friend had moved to New York, and she was an artist. She and Yolen quickly put together several little picture books. One was an alphabet book of names, one was a book about kite flying, and one was about a whale who wished to be a minnow (a tiny fish). Yolen also wrote two proposals (outlines) for longer books—one about kite flying and one about female pirates.

A Disappointing Beginning

The editor did not buy any of Yolen's little books, but she did give her some advice and put her in touch with another editor who handled children's books. Yolen then sent her books out to editor after editor, only to have them all returned. According to Yolen, "Rejection, in person or by letter, is never easy to take. But it is one of the constants in the world of publishing and anyone too shaken in confidence by a first refusal (or a second or a twenty-second) will never make it in the writing world."[2]

Then Yolen's father put her in touch with a friend of his who happened to be the vice president of a publishing company, who in turn put her in touch with an editor, who in turn put her in touch with a children's editor named Rose Dobbs. When Yolen met with Dobbs, the woman made one thing very clear: She never bought books from unknown writers. And Yolen, at this point, was as unknown as a writer could get. Dobbs dismissed all the picture books Yolen showed her, but she paused over the proposal for the book about female pirates and asked her to let her think about it for a few weeks.

After a few weeks stretched into months with no word from Dobbs, Yolen decided that she'd better find a paying job. Eventually, she found a job at Gold Medal Books, a publishing firm that specialized in westerns and spy thrillers. Eventually, Yolen was allowed to write cutlines, the one-liners on book jackets that say something brief and tempting about the book, like "He was the one who almost got away . . . with murder!" and "They never knew love could be this dangerous." Yolen's most famous cutline, which she wrote for a romance novel, reads, "She was all things to two men."[3] Imagine the book that inspired that quote.

Happy Birthday to Jane Yolen

On her twenty-second birthday—February 11, 1961—Yolen heard from Rose Dobbs, who had decided to buy Yolen's book *Pirates in Petticoats*. Yolen rushed out of Dobbs's office and then over to the club where she knew her father would be having lunch and gave him the good news.

"Not every author's story of a first book goes like that," Yolen wrote in an article. "It is rare, indeed, that an editor buys a synopsis from an unknown. But Rose Dobbs took a chance that

Pirates in Petticoats would turn into a solid book. And though the book is out of print now and Rose may be dead, it was her willingness to sit down with a young writer a year later and go over the completed manuscript, word by word by word, that started me on the path of publication."[4]

Yolen continued to work at Gold Medal Books for a while, then left for a job at Rutledge Press, where she met a woman named Frances Keene. Keene left soon after to become editor in chief of the children's book department at Macmillan, another large publishing house. Keene expressed interest in Yolen's story ideas, and thereafter a productive professional relationship began. "Keene (as she preferred to be called) was a great teacher as well as a fine editor," Yolen said. "She taught me to trust my storytelling ability and to work against being too quick . . . She also pushed me into delving deeply into folklore while at the same time recognizing my comedic talents."[5] Eventually, Keene published five of Yolen's books.

Yolen ended up leaving Rutledge Press for a position as an assistant editor in the children's department at Knopf. Yolen spent three years in this position, learning about the business of children's book publishing and perfecting her craft. In this position, she wrote the jacket copy (the paragraph on the back of the book that tells what the book is about) for many famous books, including Roald Dahl's classic story *Charlie and the Chocolate Factory* (1964) and for many other not-so-famous books. (By the way, while she was working as an assistant editor, Yolen got to meet Roald Dahl, whom she described as "very tall, mysterious, imperious [authoritative or bossy], and funny.")[6]

According to Yolen, during this period she was writing all the time, as much as possible. And although she'd nearly stopped writing poetry altogether, a certain amount of poetry was sneaking into her stories—sometimes as chants or songs.

Love Changes Everything

The second thing that happened during the year after Yolen graduated from college is that one night, at a crowded housewarming party Yolen threw with her roommates, a man who didn't want to wait in line to get into the apartment sneaked in through an open window.

As Yolen later recalled, "[The man] saw me standing in the crowd, my long braid over one shoulder, and came over, kissed me on the nape of the neck, and introduced himself.

"'I'm David Stemple,' he said, with a slow smile. 'I'm a friend of one of the girls who lives here.'"[7]

It was a slow friendship and a lengthy courtship, but in 1962, David and Jane were married in the garden of her parents' home. They remain married to this day.

Also that year, while Yolen was writing cutlines for Rutledge Press, she and David lived in a small apartment in the East Village in New York City. David was working with computers at IBM. After five years, they started feeling restless, and they decided to do something very adventurous and not a little scary—their plan was to save up a lot of money, quit their jobs, sell all their furniture, buy a camper bus (a car you can sleep in), and travel around Europe until their money ran out.

And that's exactly what they did.

Says Yolen of Stemple, "He was the perfect partner for a yearlong camping trip. Slow to anger, with a wicked sense of the absurd, a fine memory for history, and the ability to speak German and workaday French, he charted our course through the cities, towns, and forests with ease."[8]

A Trip to Remember

Yolen took her typewriter along on their adventure, and she tried to write something every day. The couple spent nine months abroad, camping in a Parisian park, the Bois de Bologne, traveling down the Rhine, and sleeping in a bed-and-breakfast hotel in Mumbles, Wales. They also spent time in museums in Spain, France, Italy, and England, picked wildflowers on top of mountains, and swam in the Mediterranean Sea. During a month spent in Italy, it seemed to David and Jane that she was sick a lot. They figured she must have picked up bronchitis in England or maybe a slight flu.

Actually, Yolen was pregnant. They received the news from a doctor in Rome, who, fortunately for them, spoke English.

They decided not to cut their trip short and continued on to Israel, where they worked for five weeks at a small kibbutz, a communal farm. From there, they sailed from Israel to Greece. Morsels of her experiences traveling in Europe have worked their ways into some of Yolen's stories—the olive grove in Greece where they spent a night became the setting of the title story in *The Girl Who Cried Flowers and Other Stories* (1974), and the sea cliffs

off the coast of Wales became the background for
Greyling (1968).

Becoming a Mother

On July 1, 1966, Yolen gave birth to her first
child, Heidi Elisabet Stemple. She also got an
agent, who began to sell her stories and books.
Yolen found that being a mother helped her
writing. Having a new baby meant spending a
lot of time sitting quietly in the dark, nursing
the child. There was nothing to do but think
and daydream. What she thought and dreamt
up became stories, and the stories began to
flow freely.

Heidi became the inspiration for several of
Yolen's characters, including Sarah in *The Gift of
Sarah Barker* (1981), Akki in the Pit Dragon
books, and Jennifer in the Tartan Magic series.
She is also the model for the little girl in *Owl
Moon* (1987), which is perhaps Yolen's most
famous picture book.

In 1968, Yolen gave birth to Adam Douglas,
and in 1970, she gave birth to Jason Frederic.
Then the family moved to Hatfield, Massachusetts, into a fourteen-room farmhouse. Later,
they bought a turn-of-the-century stone house in

Saint Andrews, Scotland. To this day, Jane and David live part-time in Hatfield and part-time in Saint Andrews, and both homes have plenty of room for Yolen to do what she does best: write stories.

3 Myths, Legends, and Folklore

In paintings and drawings, what objects are mermaids usually holding in their hands? How did Arthur prove to the world that he was really king? What color is a unicorn's hide? What gift did Prometheus give to humanity? What color was Paul Bunyan's four-legged friend?

Maybe some of these names sound familiar to you. Perhaps you've seen pictures of unicorns or cartoons about singing mermaids. And maybe you've heard of King Arthur and Paul Bunyan, but you don't remember exactly who they were or why they became famous. Well, all of these characters—mermaids, unicorns, King Arthur, Paul

Folklore in Popular Culture

Folklore—also called legend or mythology—is the basis for all modern stories. Every culture—ancient Greek and Roman, Japanese, Scandinavian, Kenyan, and so on—has folklore in its history. And various cultures' folklores aren't as different from one another as you might think. Folklore has its roots in the oral tradition, which means that the stories were circulated out loud, like ghost stories told around a campfire.

Everywhere you look in popular culture today, you can see the influence of folklore. Without Diana, the Roman goddess of the moon and the hunt, and the Amazons—the tribe of Greek women who lived separately from men and burned off their breasts to better handle bows and arrows—there would be no Bionic Woman or Wonder Woman. Without Paul Bunyan, the legendary Minnesotan logger, there would be no Incredible Hulk. In Spider-Man, we can see the legend of Anansi, the West African trickster spider, as well as Robin Hood, the English outlaw who robbed from the rich and gave to the poor.

Before there were superheroes, there were folk heroes.

Bunyan, and Greek gods like Prometheus—are characters in a long, timeless collection of stories called folklore.

When reading Jane Yolen's tales, one is constantly reminded of a tradition of storytelling that existed long before her time. Her stories are filled with legends and lore, and even if folk legends aren't mentioned by name, common themes and story lines find their way into her work. King Arthur's magician friend, Merlin, for example, appears in *Merlin and the Dragons* (1995) and the Young Merlin Trilogy—a group of three books that all involve the same story or characters (*Hobby*, 1992; *Passager*, 1996; and *Merlin*, 1997). Folkloric themes of transformation, moral goodness defeating evil, and family bonds can be found in almost all of Yolen's stories.

In a recent interview, Yolen talked about her particular appreciation for Merlin, the original magician. She said, "There is a genderless, ageless quality to Merlin that fascinates me. He is male, but does not seem male. He is very androgynous"—having both female and male characteristics—"for most of his life. His magic is art. He's a fantasy character because he can do real magic, not just sleight of hand. And he is the very best at what he does."[1]

Unicorns—another legendary creature—appear in Yolen's books *Here There Be Unicorns* (1994) and *Transfigured Hart* (1975). Dragons, which are mentioned in legends dating back to 2000 BC and are used to represent sin and destruction, crop up in Yolen's Pit Dragon Trilogy (*Dragon's Blood*, 1982; *Heart's Blood*, 1984; and *A Sending of Dragons*, 1987). In this trilogy, the main dragon helps her master, Jakkin, to break out of a life of slavery, then saves his life and the life of his friend, Akki. For Yolen, the dragon is not only a symbol of sin and destruction, but also of its opposite: the human potential to overcome adversity.

About her interest in mythology, Yolen says, "One of the first stories that I ever remember reading was the Arthurian story. I read it in *The Book of Wonder*, an encyclopedia belonging to my parents. It was not organized alphabetically; it was organized in stories. When I was about seven or eight years old, I started from the first volume, and I read all the way through. The Arthurian story just absolutely transfixed me, and I believed that it was the greatest and most wonderful story that was ever told."[2]

Neptune Rising: Songs and Tales of the Undersea Folk (1982, out of print) is Yolen's collection of stories about legends of the sea. These stories contain mermaids and mermen, selkies (seal people who can shed their seal skins on land), undines (female water sprites who can acquire souls by marrying human beings), and the sea gods, like Neptune himself, for whom the eighth planet from the sun is named.

Neptune's eight moons are named for sea legends as well, including Nereid, which was named for the sea nymph daughters of the Greek god Nereus, and Triton, which was named for the son of the Greek sea god, Poseidon. This is just one example of how classical mythology influences everyday modern life. If you haven't studied Greek and Roman mythology in school, you might want to check out a book about it from your local library—otherwise, there's no telling what you might miss.

Ancient Myths, Abridged

If you can learn even some of the classic legends and tales—from Arthurian legend to Greek and Roman myths to the Grimm brothers' fairy tales—you'll be on your way to understanding how stories work, what themes occur over and over again, and how ancient culture has influenced modern culture. See if you can find the answers to the questions at the beginning of this chapter in the following paragraphs about some popular myths and legends.

Mermaids are supernatural creatures made of the upper bodies of beautiful women and the lower bodies of scaly, iridescent fish. Mermaids often tell the future and fall in love with humans. In many tales, mermaids are depicted combing their long hair with one hand and holding a mirror with the other.

Arthur, the son of King Uther Pendragon and Lady Ygraine, was given away as an infant by the magician Merlin to a man named Hector. Arthur is raised by Hector's son, Kay, as a commoner in a village. He is not revealed to be the rightful king until he succeeds at a test devised by King Uther to choose his successor: Arthur pulls a sword from a stone. Arthur later marries Guinevere, who falls in love with a knight named Lancelot, and the story goes on from there—full of twists and turns and surprises.

Unicorns, which were often depicted in tapestries in the Middle Ages, are muscular, powerful horselike creatures who have a long, twisted horn in the middle of their foreheads. Traditionally, unicorns are all white in color.

Prometheus, whose name means forethought, and Epimetheus, whose name means afterthought, were given the task of creating humanity and giving humans and animals all the gifts they would need to survive. Epimetheus spent all his resources giving the animals strength, speed, feathers, fur, and courage, so it was up to Prometheus to make humans superior to animals. First he gave humans the ability to walk upright, then he journeyed to the sun and lit a torch with it; it was Prometheus who gave humans the gift of fire.

Paul Bunyan, an incredibly strong logger, left his mark on the American landscape by forging Puget Sound in Washington State, the Grand Canyon in Arizona, and the Black Hills in Wyoming and South Dakota. Paul Bunyan never worked without his blue ox, Babe, who was known to haul whole forests at a time.

There's more where that came from. See the For Further Reading list at the back of this book for places you can go to learn more about classic folklore. And pick up a few of Jane Yolen's novels to see how an author as well versed in folklore as she is uses her knowledge to create stories that are suspenseful, comic, affecting, and, above all, timeless.

Remaking Modern Folklore

Though she is equally comfortable writing fiction or nonfiction, stories or poems, books for kids or books for adults, Jane Yolen has written more picture books and middle school and young adult novels than any other kinds. *Owl Moon*, her most popular picture book, won a Caldecott Medal in 1988 for illustrator John Schoenherr, and another popular picture book, *The Emperor and the Kite*, was a Caldecott Honor Book in 1968. (The is one of the most important awards given to books written for children.) *Owl Moon* was based on her husband and daughter, who make a habit of watching owls together, and *The Emperor and the Kite* was influenced by Yolen's father's passion for flying kites.

All in all, Yolen has written approximately forty-five middle-grade and young adult novels to date. Some, like the Pit Dragon Trilogy, are purely fantasy novels—these books are set on a fictional planet called Austar IV—and some contain only a note of fantasy, like *The Devil's Arithmetic* (1988), a novel set mostly in Germany during the Holocaust.

The Devil's Arithmetic is perhaps Yolen's most well-known book, partly because it was made into a television movie in 1999 starring film actress Kirsten Dunst, who also starred in the films *Bring It On* (2000) and *Spider-Man* (2002). Also, the book was very popular with young readers and critics alike.

The Devil's Arithmetic is about a Jewish teenager named Hannah Stern who lives in the United States and who, like Yolen herself at that age, was having a difficult time learning and remembering so much about Jewish history and ritual. At a family seder (pronounced SAY-der), which is a traditional ceremonial meal at Passover, she finds herself transported back in time to a shtetl, a small Jewish village, in Poland during the Holocaust. She is then taken with her fellow villagers to a concentration camp and learns why it is important to study and understand history. The story is suggestive of other famous stories where girls find themselves magically transported to different places and times, like *The Wizard of Oz* (1900) and *Alice in Wonderland* (1865).

According to Yolen, *The Devil's Arithmetic* was the first book for kids to show what it might have been like to be a young person living in a concentration camp. The reviews were very good. As Yolen explains to her readers, "I had thought about doing a book on the Holocaust for a long time, but quite frankly the idea overwhelmed me. Finally one of my editors, who was a rabbi's wife, persuaded me the time had come to confront the task. Writers and storytellers are the memory of a civilization, and we who are alive now really must not forget what happened in that awful time or else we may be doomed to repeat it."[3] The research and writing of *The Devil's Arithmetic* took her many years to complete. When she was finished, she promised she would never write another book about the Holocaust because the process was so emotionally draining.

However, breaking her promise to herself, Yolen wrote another novel about the Holocaust, this time for adults. This book is called *Briar Rose* (1992) and is set at a concentration camp inside a castle.

Many of Yolen's books are based on historical events, like *Queen's Own Fool* (2000, coauthored by Robert J. Harris), which is a historical account of the tragic and thrilling life of Mary Queen of Scots, narrated by one of her three sisters. *The Gift of Sarah Barker* (1981, out of print), is set in a Shaker community in New England in the 1850s. *Children of the Wolf* (1984) is based on the true story of the Midnapore Wolf Girls, Amala and Kamala, who were found in a wolf's den in Midnapore, India, in the 1920s and moved to an orphanage. Later, Yolen coauthored a nonfiction book about the same incident with her daughter, Heidi. That book is called *The Wolf Girls: An Unsolved Mystery from History* (2001).

Like mythology and history, religion is an essential part of culture and therefore appears in stories told throughout time. Not surprisingly, religious themes have often worked their ways into Yolen's books, too. For example, *The Gift of Sarah Barker* is about the Shakers, and *The Devil's Arithmetic* is about Judaism today and during the Holocaust. Yolen has also written stories, children's books, and poems about angels and Jewish holidays.

One of Yolen's most religious books is *Armageddon Summer* (1968), which is not about

Catholicism or Quakerism or Judaism—it's about a religious group that believes the world is going to end. As previously mentioned, Yolen wrote *Armageddon Summer* with writer Bruce Coville. They wrote alternating chapters from the points of view of a girl and a boy whose parents have followed a charismatic religious leader named Reverend Beelson to the top of a mountain, where the group is awaiting the destruction of the planet.

Coville wrote the chapters that are told from the point of view of Jed, a young boy whose father has grown desperate and lonely since being abandoned by his wife. The chapters Yolen wrote were written from the point of view of Marina, a young girl who greatly wants to believe in the cult, because that belief might save her family. This book embodies traditional themes of religious belief, longing for community, and family loyalty that are found in stories throughout history and across cultures. The story also revolves around the romance between Jed and Marina, a romance that ultimately has the power to accomplish everything the characters want to accomplish, including saving their families and their own lives.

4 A Sense of Jane Yolen's Writing Style

Yolen's prose, or writing style, is simple and clear, with obvious attention paid to how words sound when read aloud. Her prose is often cited for its poetic rhythm, and she is known throughout the publishing world—not to mention among her many fans—for her rhyming skills and sense of humor. She is also known for her skills of characterization—the development of each character throughout the course of a story or novel. Even when the subject of her story is grim, as is the case with the Holocaust setting of *The Devil's Arithmetic*, Yolen's passion for telling stories is always evident in her lively language. Her books read like she sat down to write one and finished it that afternoon, as if the story came to her altogether in one long yarn, as opposed to bits and pieces.

About Yolen's collection of stories, *The Girl Who Cried Flowers and Other Tales* (1974), one reviewer said, "Yolen's artistry with words . . . makes a striking book. These could be called modern folk- or fairy tales, since they [contain] all the usual ingredients—supernatural beings, inexplicable happenings, the struggle between good and evil forces."[1]

As previously mentioned, Yolen is equally comfortable writing short stories or novels, poems or nonfiction, for young children or young adults. Whatever the genre, her style is always natural and elegant, meaning that readers have a hard time putting down her work once they pick it up. If she's writing stories and novels, the plots are spellbinding and the tension high. If she's writing poetry, the images are powerful and clear. If she's writing nonfiction, the information she provides is interesting and unique to her subject. Her stories, novels, poems, and nonfiction share a respect for traditional storytelling methods and for strong moral characters.

Take, for example, the following excerpt from *The Emperor and the Kite* (1967):

Once in ancient China there lived a princess
who was the fourth daughter of the emperor.
She was very tiny. In fact she was so tiny that
her name was Djeow Seow, which means "the
smallest one." And, because she was so tiny,
she was not thought very much of—when she
was thought of at all.[2]

Note how the opening line of the book
resembles the opening line of a fairy tale. Right
away, Yolen has created a story where the
reader identifies with the emperor's young
daughter, especially in the last sentence; as
readers, we can't help but feel a little sorry for
the girl, which means we care about what happens to her. Regarding Yolen's language in *The
Emperor and the Kite*, one reviewer said, "Here
is a writer who delights in words and can use
them in a controlled way to beautiful effect,
and a style that accords well with the ancient
Chinese setting."[3]

When Yolen edited a collection of folktales
called *Favorite Folktales from Around the World*
(1988), she selected and wrote down many stories that traditionally have been told out loud.
In the introduction to the collection, she
explains the difference between reading stories
out loud and writing them down.

There are stories [taken] from the lips of a storyteller that die miserably on the page. But other stories, set down by a particularly able transcriber, actually take on greater life in a book. And some stories are born directly in print and suffer from being spoken aloud, though they may trace a common ancestor back to the oral tradition. Perhaps it would be wiser to say that there are some stories meant only to be read and some meant only to be heard, and some that are felicitous [pleasing] to either eye or ear.[4]

But Yolen pays as much attention to character as she does language. As previously mentioned, Yolen's novel *Armageddon Summer* is about two teenagers who meet and fall in love when their parents drag them into a religious cult that believes that the world is about to end. The teens are torn between loyalty to their parents and mistrust of the cult leader, Reverend Beelson. A review of the book in *School Library Journal* called *Armageddon Summer* "a gripping and compelling tale."[5]

Another review in *Fantasy and Science Fiction* magazine stated, "There are no easy answers in this novel, and there are no simple characterizations; both writers [coauthors Jane Yolen and

Bruce Coville] are skilled enough to paint a full picture even through the narrow experience and tangled affections of their narrators. It was a lovely piece of work, but only a simple one if you don't look beyond the surface."[6]

Some readers and critics have expressed disappointment with the ending of *Armageddon Summer*, which is more or less happy. But as the above critic pointed out, the situation Yolen creates is a unique and challenging one. Yolen and Coville took turns writing chapters for the novel, which begins with Yolen's character, Marina, a young girl who is brought into the cult by her mother. Here is an excerpt from the first chapter of the novel.

> It all began at dinner one night last fall, when Mom announced, right after grace, "I've had a revelation."
>
> It was so astonishing no one moved, not even to pass the macaroni and cheese. We just sat there waiting to hear the rest.
>
> "I'm going to teach the children at home," Mom said.
>
> "Myrna," Dad told her, "that revelation only reveals that you're tired of cleaning houses."

"It's true that cleaning someone else's slop is awful," she said, "when I've got so much of my own at home. But that's not the true reason. The true reason is that Reverend Beelson says that the schools are corrupting our children and those who are corrupted will burn in the fires of Hell."

Well, that started our own little version of Hell. Mom and Dad began to snipe at each other like soldiers on a personal battlefield, the worst fight ever. It was so awful Leo started to cry. I grabbed him up and took him out onto the porch rocker. I sang him lullabies—"All the Pretty Little Horses" and "Dance to Your Daddy" and "Rock-a-Bye, Baby"—all of which he still loved, though he was way past three.[7]

Right away, Yolen has created a tense atmosphere full of unresolved issues. Already, by the end of the first page of the novel, the reader is given a lot of information: that the family is on the verge of a major change, and that the narrator—the person telling the story—is the big sister and she takes care of her younger brother. Yolen's style is easy to follow, and the pacing is rapid. Right from the beginning, the situations she creates are lively and tense.

While the setting of *Armageddon Summer* might not be familiar to most readers—on top of a mountain, inside a religious cult—some of Yolen's other books are even farther removed from reality. For example, *Dragon's Blood* (1982), one book in the Pit Dragon series, is set on the fictional planet Austar IV, and involves a young servant named Jakkin who hopes to obtain his freedom by stealing a dragon hatchling and training it to fight. Throughout the Pit Dragon series, Yolen incorporates elements of science fiction, and the series was praised for its complete fulfillment of an imaginary world. One critic called the book an "original and engrossing fantasy,"[8] while another critic described the novel as "a fascinating glimpse of a brand new world."[9]

The following is an excerpt from *Dragon's Blood*, which highlight's Yolen's instinctive feel for suspense and her use of clear language.

> Jakkin thought, and not for the first time, how his inability to sense anything in the egg made stealing a dragon so difficult. Eggs were never counted; hatchlings were. That was because so few of the eggs actually hatched. Anyone could steal an egg unnoticed. But unless the thief could sense the living dragon within the shell, his chances for success were small.[10]

Another interesting note about the Pit Dragon series is that even though the characters and setting may seem far-fetched, they are always described in realistic ways. Also, young Jakkin confronts some of the same issues that challenge teenagers today, such as drug addiction and sexuality.

The characters in Yolen's most famous book, *The Devil's Arithmetic* (1988), also confront difficult challenges—but this time, the challenges are based on historical events. As previously mentioned, the main character, Hannah, in *The Devil's Arithmetic*, travels back in time during her family's Passover dinner and finds herself imprisoned in a concentration camp. A reviewer for *Kirkus Reviews*, a journal that reviews books, wrote, "Yolen is the author of a hundred books, many of which have been praised for their originality, humor, or poetic vision, but this thoughtful, compelling novel is unique among them."[11] And there's no doubt that Yolen has a talent for making her characters and settings seem realistic on the printed page. Another reviewer noted that in *The Devil's Arithmetic*, the depictions of the horrors of the concentration camp are "more graphic than any we've seen in holocaust fiction for children before."[12]

The following excerpt from *The Devil's Arithmetic* illustrates Yolen's direct and persuasive writing style. Though there are no dragons in this story, it contains the same attention to detail that characterizes all of Yolen's books. Pay attention to her ability to build suspense, her subtle use of humor, and the way she describes what might be an unfamiliar religious ceremony.

Aaron's hands shook and a page in the Haggadah flipped over by itself. Hannah reached out and smoothed it back for him and he smiled at her gratefully. He has the greatest smile, Hannah thought. He won't need braces.

"Stop worrying," she mouthed at him.

At her urging, he plunged into the Second Question, chanting the Hebrew perfectly because he'd memorized it. But when he looked down at the book to read the English translation, he stumbled over the word herb, pronouncing the *h*. Uncle Sam snorted and Aaron stopped, mortified. He looked around the table. Everyone was smiling at him. It was clear he'd made some silly mistake, but he didn't know what it was he'd done. He turned helplessly to Hannah.

"Erb," she corrected with a whisper. "Don't pronounce the *h*."

He nodded gratefully and started on the English again, finishing too loudly and in a rush, a sure sign he was unhappy. "On all other nights we eat vegetables and 'erbs of all kinds. Why on this night do we eat bitter 'erbs especially?"

Why indeed, Hannah wondered. Since they're so disgusting. Rosemary gets to eat jelly beans and I get to eat horseradish. "It isn't fair!" She realized suddenly that she'd spoken the last words out loud and everyone had heard. Embarrassed, she stared down at her hands, but her anger at the injustice continued.

"Of course it isn't fair," whispered Aunt Eva to her, "but what has fair got to do with it?" She smiled and, to break the tension, started singing "Dayenu" in her strong, musical voice. The rousing repetitive song carried them all along, even Hannah's mother, who was tone deaf.[13]

The story follows the traditions and rituals of the Passover evening, always describing each step clearly and in detail, until, late in the dinner, the story takes on a spooky tone. As with many suspenseful novels, Yolen ends chapters with cliffhangers, which keep readers wondering what will happen next.

The Gift of Sarah Barker (1981), another historical novel, is set in a Shaker community in the

1850s. The book illustrates what Shaker life was like through the eyes of two teenagers. One reviewer called the novel "bittersweet" and "rich in fact-based detail." Some mild criticism accompanied the praise: "While the personal dynamics of the story could have been more fully developed, Yolen effectively individualizes her characters and evokes a vivid image . . . of a Shaker haven."[14]

Another review stated, "This is an absorbing tale . . . Even the minor characters are rounded personalities!"[15] Unlike some historical fiction, readers don't need to know anything about the Shaker movement to follow the story or even to be interested in what happens. All of Yolen's books follow the lives of likable, realistic characters who have qualities shared by most teenagers today, no matter what the setting is or during what period the story takes place.

Whether your taste runs toward the imaginary or the real, Yolen's writing style is easy to follow, humorous, suspenseful, and straightforward, and the situations she creates are vivid and exciting. Her characters—even those who reside on distant, imaginary planets—are thoughtful, gentle, intelligent, and caring, not to mention adventurous. Yolen's stories follow youthful detectives, friendly dragons, wizards, knights, explorers, and other characters—realistic and fantastical—through time and space, with plenty of plot twists and suspense to keep even the most distracted readers on the edge of their seats.

5 Recipe for Success

Jane Yolen writes every day. She sits for several hours at her computer and makes sure she gets something—anything—down on the page before she gets up again. As she explains, "My writing begins at 6:30 in the morning with a quick scan of e-mail and a cup of tea in my attic writing room . . . It is a wonderful sanctuary for me. Except for food and potty breaks, and time to answer the phone and get the mail, the rest of my day—often until five in the evening—is taken up with writing. As William Faulkner said: 'I only write when I am inspired. Fortunately, I am inspired at nine o'clock every morning.' For me,

61

writing is both work and pleasure and I am very focused . . ."[1]

In fact, Yolen doesn't understand why some writers say they find writing to be a painful exercise. In an interview reprinted in 1997, Yolen said, "I'm spending all day, every day—[except] holidays—writing. Well, I must admit, the day my granddaughter was born, ten months ago, I didn't write. I write on the road. I write all the time. Why on earth would anyone who found the process painful do it all the time . . .?"[2]

When she is writing, Yolen frequently feels as if she is "transported" to the time and place where her story takes place. Often, the ringing telephone or the sound of the doorbell will interrupt her, and she will be surprised to find herself back at home, in the twenty-first century, at her writing desk.

Talking to Elves and Overcoming Writer's Block

Yolen rarely knows where her characters are headed when she imagines them for the first time. As she stated in an interview, "I keep on writing because I want to know what is going to happen to my characters. I've had a book in which a bunch of elves walked in, and I said, 'No elves in this book.' And they said, 'We're here.' And I said, 'No, you're not. Go away.' And I was blocked for three weeks until I figured out why they were there. So sometimes characters simply walk on and sort of have squatters' rights until you figure it out."[3]

Generally, though, Yolen doesn't believe in that horrible problem called writer's block—the failure to get words onto the page—that affects almost all writers, making it impossible for them to get any work done. Instead of giving into writer's block, Yolen has developed a remedy for it: She always works on more than one project at one time. In fact, she has been known to work on as many as ten or twelve books at once. "But some of them are very much in the foreground and some of them are in the [background]—everything is not right up front clamoring for the same kind of attention,"[4] she said.

About her own writing process, Yolen says, "Some people are pony express writers: They get on one horse and ride it until they get where they're going. Some are able to hook two matched bays together and drive them to the finish line . . . I'm a mule-train driver: I hook up twenty-four of these little suckers [ideas], and maybe one of them dies along the way, and I cut it out . . . and keep going. So, by the time I get to the end, I've got twenty-three!"[5]

Yolen emphasizes that in order to keep as many as twenty-four ideas going at once, a writer needs to learn to prioritize. "As a young writer," she says, "I thought all my ideas equally viable and valuable. Now I know better and tend my aging garden with care."[6] If she loses momentum on one project, she switches to another until that one, too, loses steam. Then she switches back. Eventually, almost everything gets finished, and she's never wasted time.

Besides the clutter on her writing desk, Yolen prefers not to have any distractions. "I am a great music lover but have to have absolute quiet while writing," she says, "because being so musical means I pick up the rhythm of whatever is playing and impose it on my prose."[7]

Yolen also likes to share her writing with her friends and has been a member and organizer of one all-female writing group for more than twenty years. The group meets regularly, shares work, and gives one another criticism. Learning to be a thoughtful and helpful critic is one essential part of being a good writer.

Enjoying the Scenery

Yolen spends most of the year in Hatfield, Massachusetts, in her big old farmhouse and her attic office, and a few months of the year in a turn-of-the-century stone house in Saint Andrews, which is located on Scotland's eastern coast, just north of the capital city, Edinburgh. In both places, Yolen writes about the same amount on a daily basis. However, in Scotland, her writing voice changes because of the way the locals speak; though they speak English in Scotland, the accent and colloquialisms are different. The landscape, too, is different and tends to affect the landscapes in her stories. Saint Andrews is located on the North Sea, and it is filled with centuries-old cathedrals and castles, historical museums, and wide green pastures.

"When I'm in Scotland," says Yolen, "I get to write. Nobody bothers me there. Nobody asks me to give a speech. Nobody knows who I am. It's great. But I don't think it's possible for a writer to retire unless you no longer have anything to write. Unless you have absolutely nothing in your head.

"I have enough ideas that if I never got another idea in my entire life, I could write for the next twenty years. And never getting another idea in my head is not an option—they just keep crowding in."[8]

Advice for Young Writers

After learning a little about Yolen's strict writing schedule, it's probably not surprising that her number one piece of advice for young writers is to write every day.

Here are some other words of advice from Jane Yolen:

1. Write what interests you.

2. Write for the child inside of you—or the adult, if you are writing adult books.

3. Write with honest emotion.

4. Be careful of being facile [doing something too easily].

5. Be wary of preaching.

6. Be prepared for serendipity [a happy or fortunate surprise].[9]

In answering some of the frequently asked questions she receives from her fans, Yolen says,

"I have three pieces of advice for young writers. One: Read, read, read! You must read every day, and try to read a wide range of books. Two: Write, write, write! Keep a journal, write letters, anything to keep the 'writing muscles' in shape. Three: Don't let anyone stop you from writing. Be persistent no matter what 'naysayers' [disbelievers] or critical editors have to say about your writing."[10]

If Yolen had let criticism dissuade her from writing, she might never have gotten past those first few meetings with editors in New York, when she was only in her early twenties, and one editor told her to learn how to write. Imagine what might have happened if she'd let *that* get the best of her!

When asked about the most common mistakes she's witnessed as a teacher of creative writing, Yolen says, "First, finishing a work is hard. Then finishing it with as much power as it was begun. Then misunderstanding that fiction should be about the growth of wisdom. Not about the writer showing off. Fourth, and probably the thing one sees most often, is a problem with transitions between scenes, between chapters."[11]

As far as style is concerned, Yolen recommends finding a style of writing you like in one of your favorite books, then trying to reproduce or imitate it. You'll almost always come out with an original writing style, even if you're not trying to.

Yolen's own experience as an aspiring writer is a good guide for young writers. After all, she was just twenty-one years old, barely out of college, living in a run-down apartment and writing half-finished poems, when an editor called her and asked if she had any completed manuscripts to show. And even though she hadn't yet written even one of her hundreds of books, what did she do? She told the editor she'd meet with her, rolled up her shirtsleeves, and got to work. Maybe Yolen didn't know her whole life that she was going to be a children's author; maybe she just believed she would be any kind of writer, perhaps a writer of long novels for adults. That day when she was twenty-one, however, when she sat down at her typewriter with only a few quickly concocted ideas for children's books, her fate was sealed. A writer—a children's writer—was born.

Parting Words

Before you read another story or novel, consider what Jane Yolen herself wrote in the *Something About the Author* series about the importance of stories and her own place in the rich cultural tradition of storytelling.

> I just want to go on writing and discovering my stories for the rest of my life because I know that in my tales I make public what is private, transforming my own joy and sadness into tales for the people. The folk.
>
> But the wonderful thing about stories is that other folk can turn them around and make private what is public; that is, they can take into themselves the story they read or hear and make it their own. Stories do not exist on the page or in the mouth, they exist between. Between writer and reader, between teller and listener.[12]

Next time you read a story, think about where that story came from, originally, and why it was passed on. And the next time you read one of Jane Yolen's books, think about the rich tradition of folklore that influenced it. You might even try to write a legend or myth of your own, using what you've learned about storytelling and folklore. A story doesn't have to be 100 percent original to be great—but it should be meaningful, entertaining, and imaginative. And it should change its reader in some subtle or dramatic way, like Hannah is changed after she meets

Elijah at the seder dinner, and like Jed and Marina are changed when they fall in love on the mountaintop.

Consider, finally, these words from Jane Yolen: "Once I received a letter from a nurse who told me that she had read the story to a dying child, and the story had eased the little girl through her final pain. The story did that—not me. But if I can continue to write with as much honesty and love as I can muster, I will truly have touched magic—and passed it on."[13]

Interview with Jane Yolen

SUSANNA DANIEL: Early on in your career, you were told by an editor not to write children's books until you'd become a mother. Do you think it is important for a children's author to have a family?

JANE YOLEN: That was perhaps the stupidest piece of advice I have ever gotten. After all, Maurice Sendak and James Marshall and Margaret Wise Brown and Beatrix Potter never had children. It is important to be in touch with the child within, the child one once was. But it is not important to raise children to write for them.

71

SUSANNA DANIEL: You write several hours a day in your attic office at home in Massachusetts and have said that you love to write. Is writing a purely joyful experience for you, or is there any part of the process that frustrates you sometimes or gets on your nerves?

JANE YOLEN: In almost every project there will be moments of frustration, when the right word or the right plot twist eludes me. But for the most part I adore the writing process. It is the publishing process, the business stuff I find infinitely frustrating.

SUSANNA DANIEL: Were you pleased with the translation of *The Devil's Arithmetic* into film? Is there anything you would have liked to see changed? Would you recommend the film to readers of your work?

JANE YOLEN: The film is strong on its own terms. But it is not the book, not entirely. And in places not even close. But that comes with the territory. In order to get it made, it had to be done with a fine young actress. Kirsten Dunst did a brilliant job—but she was already four years older than my hero, Hannah Chaya. So the changes began.

SUSANNA DANIEL: You've said that you believe folklore is all but missing from contemporary children's education. If you had to choose three important legends or tales for all children to learn, which would they be?

JANE YOLEN: First, there is a major difference between legends (stories that are said to have historical content) and tales. But if I look at folklore and myth in particular, I would like children to be conversant with the great Greco-Roman mythology on which so much of Western culture is based. I would hope they would know the Bible (as literature, not necessarily as religion). And the great collections of stories, such as the Grimms' and the Afanasev's Russian stories, the Jacobs English and Celtic stories, et cetera. Know them as great stories. Have them in the bones. Likewise the collections of African, Native American, et cetera. And then of course the Arthurian canon.

SUSANNA DANIEL: You've written folktales, poems, short stories, and novels. What are the advantages and disadvantages of telling stories in each genre?

JANE YOLEN: Hmmm . . . not a question I can answer without writing a book. In fact, I have a book on writing coming out in the spring [of 2003] that answers that—*Take Joy* (Kalmbach Press).

SUSANNA DANIEL: You've told the story of how difficult it was for you to break into publishing children's books—and how lucky you were along the way. In your opinion, how much of becoming successful depends on persistence and discipline, and how much depends on passion?

JANE YOLEN: Passion and persistence and luck are equal. Talent is the smallest part of the equation.

SUSANNA DANIEL: Before your first child was born, you and your husband, David, traveled together in Europe for almost a year. How has traveling affected your work, and would you recommend traveling to young people who are interested in writing stories?

JANE YOLEN: Traveling is my passion. But others who stay at home (because they want to or have to) have written wonderfully. Rosemary Sutcliffe is a primary example. One has to be a passionate observer, not necessarily a traveler, to be a writer.

SUSANNA DANIEL: Do you read reviews of your own work? Do you have any practical advice for handling negative criticism?

JANE YOLEN: Yes, I read them. And I handle negative notices badly. I curse. I take a hot shower. And then I get back to work.

SUSANNA DANIEL: You've said that you were a writer from the time you could write. Do you think this is true of most writers? Do you have advice for young people who haven't found their special talents or interests?

JANE YOLEN: My closest writing friend, a woman who has won the Newbery, didn't start writing till she was in her early forties—Patricia MacLachlan. So age doesn't matter

SUSANNA DANIEL: If you could return to seventh grade, knowing what you know now, what would you do differently?

JANE YOLEN: Eat better, exercise more, study harder, take voice lessons, practice the piano every day without complaint.

SUSANNA DANIEL: Were there times in your life when you thought about not writing anymore? What is your advice for young people who feel like giving up on their ambitions?

JANE YOLEN: I could no more stop writing than stop breathing, so I cannot answer this. Except to say that if you give up on your ambition, it wasn't important enough to you.

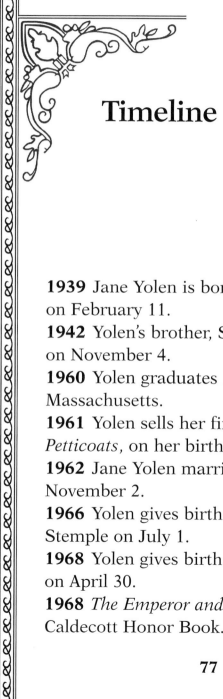

Timeline

1939 Jane Yolen is born in New York City on February 11.

1942 Yolen's brother, Steven Hyatt, is born on November 4.

1960 Yolen graduates from Smith College in Massachusetts.

1961 Yolen sells her first book, *Pirates in Petticoats,* on her birthday.

1962 Jane Yolen marries David Stemple on November 2.

1966 Yolen gives birth to Heidi Elisabet Stemple on July 1.

1968 Yolen gives birth to Adam Douglas on April 30.

1968 *The Emperor and the Kite* is named a Caldecott Honor Book.

1970 Yolen gives birth to Jason Frederic on May 21.

1975 *The Transfigured Hart* is named a Golden Kite honor book by the Society of Children's Book Writers and Illustrators.

1976 Yolen earns a master's degree in education from the University of Massachusetts.

1988 *Owl Moon* wins a Caldecott Medal in 1988 for illustrator John Schoenherr.

1990 *Sister Light, Sister Dark* wins the Nebula Award, which is given every year by the Science Fiction Fantasy Writers of America.

1999 *The Devil's Arithmetic* is made into a film starring actress Kirsten Dunst.

Selected Reviews from *School Library Journal*

Boots and the Seven Leaguers:
A Rock-and-Troll
October 2000

Gr 5–8—It's three days until Boots and the Seven Leaguers, the greatest Rock-and-Troll band in the world, will play their annual concert at Rhymer's Bridge, and Gog, their biggest fan, has no coins for tickets. With the genius of his little brother, Magog, and the trickery of his best friend, Pook, Gog and Pook manage to land the roadie jobs that will earn them seats at the concert. But while they are working, Magog is kidnapped. Gog and Pook must enter the New Forest and match wits with the Weed King, resist the temptation of a deadly woodwife, outhunt the Huntsman, and brave the Great White Wyrm. This contemporary tale will introduce readers to a Kingdom that has kept up with a modern age. The story carries the characters quickly from one fantastical adventure to the next, and initiates readers to new customs and peculiarities of the Kingdom as it goes. Gog and Pook are as crass and cool as any teenage boys. They and the other denizens of the Kingdom will amuse and engage readers as they are entangled in the author's spell. A well-crafted and exciting tale. —Heather Dieffenbach, Lexington Public Library, Kentucky

Girl in a Cage
2002

Gr 6–10—The coauthors of *Queen's Own Fool* (Philomel, 2000) present an equally compelling interpretation of an earlier period in Scotland's history told by another young protagonist. In 1306, a year has passed since patriot William "Braveheart" Wallace was executed, and things are not going well for the cause of Scottish freedom. Robert Bruce, newly crowned king of Scotland, has managed to evade his powerful enemy, Edward I of England, but many allies have been killed or taken. A recent capture is Bruce's eleven-year-old daughter, Marjorie. The princess finds herself conveyed to the English border town of Lanercost, locked in an iron cage, and displayed outdoors day and night by the decree of ailing King Edward, "Longshanks," himself. Marjorie's first-person narration of her captivity and the events leading up to it are exciting and moving, and her strategies for coping with a hideous imprisonment are models of ingenuity and staying true to oneself. The time line and afterword are helpful in understanding the historical context within which the authors place their well-wrought fictional tale. —Starr E. Smith, Fairfax County Public Library, Virginia

Here There Be Ghosts
Illustrated by David Wilgus
1998

Gr 5 Up—Ghosts, lost souls, and demented prom dates roam the pages in this collection of new and previously published short stories and poems by the prolific author. Each entry is prefaced by a note by Yolen discussing the origin of the piece and her thoughts about it. These comments will be useful when introducing poetry and stories, providing background information, and aiding in interpretation. However, the insights offered often give away essential information and would be best read after completing the selection. Soft pencil drawings illustrate this addition to the author's "Here There Be . . ." series (Harcourt). Readers will do some serious thinking about topics such as God, souls, and the supernatural while devouring these creepy tales. —Kimberlie Baker, Lucius Beebe Memorial Library, Wakefield, Massachusetts

Here There Be Witches
Illustrated by David Wilgus
1995

Gr 4–8—A fine companion volume to *Here There Be Dragons* (1993, Harcourt) and *Here There Be Unicorns* (1994, Harcourt). Seven poems and ten short stories present views of witches that range from humorous to poignant. A boy from a long line of sorcerers completes a routine homework assignment in "When I Grow Up, by Michael Dee." Yolen takes a sly poke at political correctness in "The Passing of the Eye," and brings Baba Yaga into the 20th century in "Boris Chernevsky's Hands." Gleanings from historical accounts serve as the seeds for "The Witch's Ride," which is about a lovely young woman beyond suspicion of witchcraft, and "Witchfinder," which takes a look at different sides of the same story. Some of the pieces have a darker note, such as "Circles," in which a young woman learns the true shape of her power, and "Weird Sisters," a poem about how some evil spells are cast by ordinary human beings. A strong, imaginative sense of story and clear, crisp language are trademarks of Yolen's work, and this collection is no exception. Wilgus's cover is enticing, and his full-page pencil drawings enhance the selections they illustrate. —Donna L. Scanlon, Lancaster County Library, Pennsylvania

O Jerusalem
Illustrated by John Thompson
April 1986

Gr 5–7—Jerusalem's holiness, history, and ageless appeal to three religions have been captured in these wonderful poems. "Abraham's Message to the Terah Clan" reads like a psalm and is as lovely. "King David's Tomb" mulls over what the city might be like had the boy David not been successful in vanquishing the giant, while "Stone upon Stone" records its successive conquerors and physical composition. "Wall 1" and "Wall 2" tell of both the

Jewish and Muslim traditions regarding the wall; "Dome of the Rock" pays obeisance to that object's importance for the three religions. In referring to the Jewish reverence for the rock, Yolen uses the Christian interpretation of Abraham's willingness to sacrifice his son (as Christ was sacrificed). The Jewish interpretation is the binding of Isaac, inferring a different meaning. The collection concludes with "Jerusalem 3000," an inspirational poem of peace. A narrative paragraph follows each poem to explain its historical references and/or allusions to legend and religion. The painterly acrylics reflect the majesty of a Jerusalem dawn, the old city panorama as seen perhaps from the Mount of Olives, black-faced sheep blending against a background of stone wall, an adolescent David contemplating his decision, and other striking perspectives. Thompson is a superb draftsman who also handles color eloquently. As each illustration is unique and a work of art, so is each poem. Together they form an integral unit and provide a most fitting celebration of the Jerusalem 3000 anniversary. —Marcia W. Posner, Holocaust Memorial and Educational Center of Nassau County, Glen Cove, New York

A Sending of Dragons
1987

Gr 7 Up—Here is the third and concluding volume in the indefatigably creative Jane Yolen's "Pit Dragon" trilogy. Jakkin and Akki, whom readers met in the two preceding volumes, have survived in the Austarian wilds through bonding with the dragon Heart's Blood, and in this volume continue their harrowing journey to freedom and spiritual enlightenment. Like the two volumes preceding it, *A Sending of Dragons'* particular strengths are in the almost encyclopedic detail which Yolen has lavished upon her fully realized alternative world of Austar IV, in her sympathetic portrayal of the dragons as both victims and telepathic partners, and in the symbolic sub-text which enriches her narrative and reinforces her universal theme of the interdependency and unique value of all life forms. Similarly the shortcomings reflect those of the two companion volumes: these include certain stylistic shortcomings and a tendency toward one-dimensional characterization. Nevertheless the trilogy remains an ambitious and rewarding work of speculative fiction. The two previous volumes should be read for a more complete

understanding and appreciation of this concluding volume. —Michael Cart, Beverly Hills Public
Library, California

Twelve Impossible Things Before Breakfast 1987

Gr 5–7—This solid collection of short stories is
a good introduction to various types of fantasy.
Three of the twelve pieces are new and the rest
have been published in other compilations.
There is something here for everyone—tales
that are scary, gross, or fanciful. Some of the
selections are reworkings of parts of children's
classics, such as *Alice in Wonderland* (Alice
learns how to be tough with the Jabberwock)
and *Peter Pan* (Captain Hook is singing a new
tune now that he is married to a modern-day
feminist). "The Bridge's Complaint" puts a different spin on "The Three Billy Goats Gruff" by
relating events from the bridge's point of view.
The tales are set in different times—some in the
past, some in the present, and some in the near
or distant future. "Wilding" is a chilling futuris-
tic look at New York City's Central Park, based
on the gang violence that occurred there in the
late 1980s. There's a story of a frightening sea
monster, one about a fairy, and another about

aliens; all will chill and delight the imagination. —Virginia Golodetz, St. Michael's College, Winooski, Vermont

List of
Selected Works

Armageddon Summer. Written with Bruce
    Coville. New York: Harcourt, 1998.
Briar Rose. New York: Tor Books, 1992.
Children of the Wolf. New York: Viking, 1984.
The Devil's Arithmetic. New York: Viking, 1988.
Dove Isabeau. Illustrated by Dennis Nolan.
    New York: Harcourt, 1989.
Dragonfield and Other Stories. New York:
    Ace Books, 1985.
Dragon's Blood: A Fantasy. New York:
    Delacorte Press, 1982.
The Dragon's Boy. New York:
    HarperCollins, 1990.
Dream Weaver and Other Tales. Illustrated by
    Michael Hague. New York: Philomel
    Books, 1989.

Eeny Up Above. Illustrated by Kathryn Brown.
New York: Harcourt, 2003.
The Emperor and the Kite. Illustrated by Ed
Young. New York: Philomel Books, 1988.
Encounter. Illustrated by David Shannon. New
York: Harcourt, 1992.
*Friend: The Story of George Fox and the
Quakers*. New York: Seabury, 1972.
The Gift of Sarah Barker. New York:
Viking, 1981.
The Girl Who Cried Flowers and Other Tales.
Illustrated by David Palladini. New York:
Crowell, 1974.
Good Griselle. Illustrated by David Christiana.
New York: Harcourt, 1994.
Grandad Bill's Song. Illustrated by Melissa Bay
Mathis. New York: Philomel Books, 1994.
Heart's Blood. New York: Delacorte Press, 1984
Here There Be Angels. New York: Harcourt, 1996.
Here There Be Dragons. New York:
Harcourt, 1993.
Here There Be Ghosts. New York: Harcourt, 1998.
Here There Be Unicorns. New York:
Harcourt, 1994.
Here There Be Witches. New York:
Harcourt, 1995.
Hobby. New York: Harcourt, 1992.

Hobo Toad and the Motorcycle Gang. New York: World Publishing, 1970.

Honkers. Illustrated by Leslie Baker. New York: Little, Brown, and Company, 1993.

How Do Dinosaurs Say Goodnight? New York: Scholastic, 2000.

Isabel's Noel. Illustrated by Arnold Roth. New York: Funk & Wagnalls, 1967.

It All Depends. Illustrated by Don Bolognese. New York: Funk and Wagnalls, 1970.

A Letter from Phoenix Farm. Photographs by Jason Stemple. Katonah, NY: Richard C. Owen, 1992.

Merlin. New York: Harcourt, 1997.

Merlin and the Dragons. Illustrated by Ming Li. New York: Dutton, 1995.

A Sending of Dragons. Illustrated by Tom McKeveny. New York: Delacorte, 1987.

Passager. New York: Harcourt, 1996.

Sister Light, Sister Dark. New York: Tor Books, 1988.

The Stone Silenus. New York: Philomel Books, 1984.

The Transfigured Hart. Illustrated by Donna Diamond. New York: Crowell, 1975.

Trust a City Kid. Illustrated by J. C. Kocsis. New York: Lothrop, 1966.

Twelve Impossible Things Before Breakfast. New York: Harcourt, 1997.

White Jenna. New York: Tor Books, 1989.

The Wild Hunt. Illustrated by Francisco Mora. New York: Harcourt, 1995.

Wizard's Hall. New York: Harcourt, 1991.

The Wizard's Map. New York: Harcourt, 1998.

World on a String: The Story of Kites. New York: World Publishing, 1968.

List of
Selected Awards

Ballad of the Pirate Queens (1995)
Bulletin of the Center for Children's Books
   Blue Ribbon (1995)

Bird Watch (1990)
Bulletin of the Center for Children's Books
   Blue Ribbon (1990)

The Devil's Arithmetic (1988)
Association of Jewish Libraries Sydney
   Taylor Book Award (1989)
Jewish Book Council Award (1989)
Nebula Award finalist, the Science Fiction/
   Fantasy Writers of America (1988)

The Emperor and the Kite (1967)
Caldecott Honor Book (1968)
Lewis Carroll Shelf Award (1968)

*Favorite Folk Tales from
Around the World* (1986)
World Fantasy Award (1987)

*The Girl Who Cried Flowers
and Other Tales* (1973)
Golden Kite Award, Society of Children's Book
Writers (1974)
American Library Association Notable
Book (1975)
National Book Award nomination (1975)

The Girl Who Loved the Wind (1972)
Children's Book Showcase of the Children's
Book Council citations (1973)
Lewis Carroll Shelf Award (1973)

The Golden Kite (1967)
New York Times Best Books of the Year (1968)

The Little Spotted Fish (1975)
Children's Book Showcase of the Children's
Book Council citations (1976)

The Moon Ribbon and Other Tales (1976)
Golden Kite Honor Book (1976)

Owl Moon (1987)
Caldecott Medal (1988)

The Seeing Stick (1977)
Christopher Medal (1977)

The Transfigured Hart (1975)
Golden Kite Honor Book, Society of Children's
    Book Writers (1975)

White Jenna (1989)
Nebula Award finalist, the Science Fiction/
    Fantasy Writers of America (1991)

World on a String: The Story of Kites (1968)
American Library Association Notable
    Book (1968)

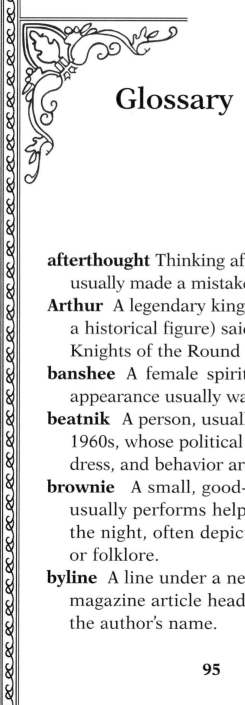

Glossary

afterthought Thinking after acting, having usually made a mistake.

Arthur A legendary king (possibly based on a historical figure) said to have led the Knights of the Round Table.

banshee A female spirit in folklore whose appearance usually warns of a death.

beatnik A person, usually of the 1950s and 1960s, whose political views, style of dress, and behavior are unconventional.

brownie A small, good-natured elf that usually performs helpful services during the night, often depicted in fairy tales or folklore.

byline A line under a newspaper or magazine article headline that provides the author's name.

courtship The period where two people get to know each other before becoming engaged to be married.

cub reporter An inexperienced reporter covering small, uncomplicated news stories.

cutline A one-liner on a book jacket that says something brief about the book.

elf A small, devious fairy, often appearing in fairy tales and folklore.

Elijah Hebrew prophet invited in spirit to join a seder, or traditional Jewish meal.

Epimetheus A figure from Greek mythology who, together with his brother Prometheus, helped form the human race. His name means afterthought.

euphonious A pleasing or sweet sound.

exodus A mass departure.

fairy tale A simple story involving imaginary figures, or fairies.

Firebird A ballet based on a tale of Russian folklore, performed by the New York City Ballet when Jane Yolen was a girl.

folklore Customs, beliefs, stories, and sayings of a culture, handed down from generation to generation.

folktale A story or legend forming part of a culture's tradition.

forethought Thinking before acting, usually preventing a mistake.

genre A particular type or category of literature.

gnome An ageless dwarf, often depicted in fairy tales and folktales, that usually guards treasure.

goblin An ugly, cunning sprite that is sometimes evil, often depicted in folklore.

Haggadah The book containing the story of the Exodus and the ritual of the seder, read at the Passover seder, a traditional meal.

hootenanny A musical gathering.

intern A worker, usually unpaid, gaining practical experience in a professional field before being hired for pay.

jacket copy A paragraph on the back of a book that explains what the book is about.

Judaism Practicing the rituals and beliefs of the Jewish faith, which developed among the ancient Hebrews.

kobold A mischievous household elf present in German folklore.

Lipizzan A breed of horses that descend from royal Austrian horses dating back to 1580, whose coats start out dark and lighten to white with age.

lyric The words of a song, or an adjective meaning poetic or easily put to music.

Merlin A prophet and magician in the legend of King Arthur.

mermaid An imaginary sea creature usually represented with a woman's body and a fish's tail.

merman An imaginary sea creature usually represented with a man's body and a fish's tail.

multicultural Relating to many cultures.

naysayers Disbelievers, or skeptics.

Neptune The god of the ocean in Roman mythology.

Nereid Any of the sea nymphs of Greek mythology; the fifty daughters of Nereus.

Nereus A Greek mythological figure of the sea; father of the Nereids.

Passover The Jewish holiday that commemorates the Hebrews' liberation from slavery in Egypt.

pixie A cheerful, mischievous sprite, often depicted in folklore.

Prometheus A Titan in Greek mythology who gives fire to human beings. His name means forethought.

prose Writing of stories or novels, lacking the repeating rhythm used in poetry.

Quaker A sect of Christianity that emphasizes human goodness and personal divinity, founded in England in the seventeenth century by a peace activist named George Fox.

seder The feast commemorating the Exodus of the Jews from Egypt, celebrated on the first night or the first two nights of Passover.

selkies Seal people found in folklore who can shed their skins on land.

shtetl A small Jewish town or village formerly found throughout eastern Europe.

sprite A disembodied spirit, often depicted in folklore.

sylph A slender, graceful woman, often depicted in folktales.

Triton A god of the sea, son of Poseidon, portrayed as having the head and trunk of a man and the tail of a fish.

undines Female water sprites found in folklore who can acquire souls by marrying human beings.

verse Poetic writing.

viable Doable or possible.

vigor Strength and enthusiasm.

For More Information

Web Sites

Due to the changing nature of Internet links, the Rosen Publishing Group, Inc., has developed an online list of Web sites related to the subject of this book. This site is updated regularly. Please use this link to access the list:

Http://www.rosenlinks.com/lab/jyol

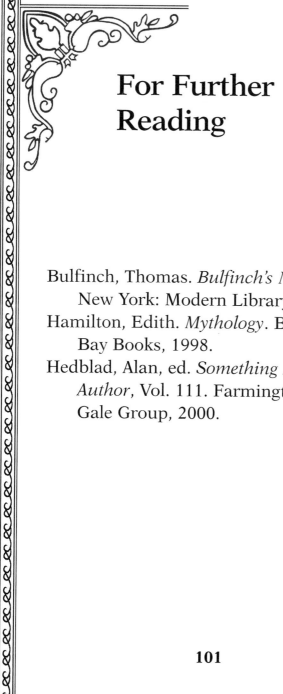

For Further Reading

Bulfinch, Thomas. *Bulfinch's Mythology.* New York: Modern Library Books, 1998.

Hamilton, Edith. *Mythology.* Boston: Back Bay Books, 1998.

Hedblad, Alan, ed. *Something About the Author*, Vol. 111. Farmington Hills, MI: Gale Group, 2000.

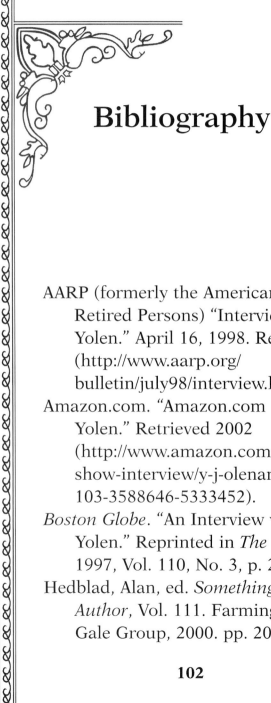

Bibliography

AARP (formerly the American Association of Retired Persons) "Interview with Jane Yolen." April 16, 1998. Retrieved 2002 (http://www.aarp.org/bulletin/july98/interview.html).

Amazon.com. "Amazon.com Talks to Jane Yolen." Retrieved 2002 (http://www.amazon.com/exec/obidos/show-interview/y-j-olenane/103-3588646-5333452).

Boston Globe. "An Interview with Jane Yolen." Reprinted in *The Writer*, March 1997, Vol. 110, No. 3, p. 20.

Hedblad, Alan, ed. *Something About the Author*, Vol. 111. Farmington Hills, MI: Gale Group, 2000. pp. 203–225.

Koch, John. "An Interview with Jane Yolen." *The Boston Globe*, April 14, 1996.

Inkspot.com. "Interview with Jane Yolen." *Inklings Newsletter*, Issue 3.17, August 20, 1997. Retrieved 2002 (http://www.inkspot.com).

Thompson, Raymond H. "Interview with Jane Yolen." Retrieved 2002 (http://www.lib.rochester.edu/camelot/intrvws/yolen.htm).

Writing. "'A Cup of Borrowed Courage': Jane Yolen on Fantasy Writing." October 2000, Vol. 23, No. 2, p. 8.

White, Clare E. "A Conversation with Jane Yolen." *Writers Write*, June 1997–2002. Retrieved 2002 (http://www.writerswrite.com/journal/jun02/yolen.htm).

Yolen, Jane. "Frequently Asked Questions." JaneYolen.com. Retrieved 2002 (http://janeyolen.com/faqs.html).

Source Notes

Introduction

1. Clare E. White, "A Conversation with Jane Yolen," *Writer's Write*, June 1997–2002, retrieved 2002 (http://www.writerswrite.com/journal/jun02/yolen.htm).
2. Ibid.

Chapter 1

1. Alan Hedblad, ed., *Something About the Author*, Vol. 111 (Farmington Hills, MI: Gale Group, 2000), pp. 203–225.
2. Ibid.
3. Ibid.
4. Ibid.
5. Ibid.
6. Ibid.
7. Ibid.

Chapter 2

1. Alan Hedblad, ed., *Something About the Author*, Vol. 111 (Farmington Hills, MI: Gale Group, 2000), pp. 203–225.
2. Ibid.
3. Ibid.
4. Ibid.
5. Ibid.
6. Ibid.
7. Ibid.
8. Ibid.

Chapter 3

1. "'A Cup of Borrowed Courage': Jane Yolen on Fantasy Writing," *Writing*, October 2000, Vol. 23, No. 2, p. 8.
2. Raymond H. Thompson, "Interview with Jane Yolen," *Interviews with Authors of Modern Arthurian Literature*, August 29, 1988. Retrieved 2002 (http://www.lib.rochester.edu/camelot/intrvws/yolen.htm).
3. Alan Hedblad, ed., *Something About the Author*, Vol. 111 (Detroit, MI: Gale Group, 2000), pp. 203–225.

Chapter 4

1. *Children's Literature Review*, Vol. 4, 1982, Vol. 16, 1989, Farmington Hills, MI: Gale Group, pp. 255–269.

2. Jane Yolen, *The Emperor and the Kite* (New York: World Publishing Company, 1967), p. 2.
3. *Children's Literature Review.*
4. Jane Yolen, ed., *Favorite Folktales from Around the World* (New York: Pantheon Books, 1988), p. 4.
5. *Children's Literature Review.*
6. Ibid.
7. Jane Yolen, *Armageddon Summer* (New York: Voyager Books, 1998), p. 1.
8. *Children's Literature Review.*
9. Ibid.
10. Jane Yolen, *Dragon's Blood* (New York: Delacorte Press, 1982), p. 6.
11. *Children's Literature Review.*
12. Ibid.
13. Jane Yolen, *The Devil's Arithmetic* (New York: Viking, 1988), pp. 14–15.
14. *Children's Literature Review.*
15. Ibid.

Chapter 5

1. Alan Hedblad, ed., *Something About the Author,* Vol. 111 (Farmington Hills, MI: Gale Group, 2000), pp. 203–225.
2. Ibid.
3. AARP. "Interview with Jane Yolen,"1989. Retrieved 2002 (http://www.aarp.org/bulletin/july98/=interview.html).

4. *Boston Globe*, "An Interview With Jane Yolen," Reprinted in *The Writer*, March 1997, Vol. 110, No. 3, p. 20.

5. Clare E. White, "A Conversation with Jane Yolen," *Writers Write*, June 1997–2002. Retrieved 2002 (http://www.writerswrite.com/journal/jun02/yolen.htm).

6. Amazon.com, "Amazon.com Talks to Jane Yolen." Retrieved 2002 (http://www.amazon.com/exec/obidos/show-interview/y-j-olenane/103-3588646-5333452).

7. AARP, "Interview with Jane Yolen."

8. White, "A Conversation with Jane Yolen."

9. Jane Yolen, "Frequently Asked Questions," Janeyolen.com, 2000. Retrieved 2002 (http://janeyolen.com/faqs.html).

10. White, "A Conversation with Jane Yolen."

11. Ibid.

12. Alan Hedblad, ed., *Something About the Author*.

13. Ibid.

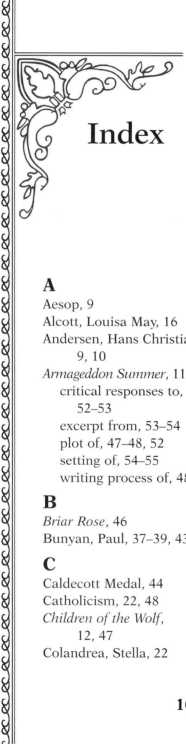

Index

Index

About the Author

Susanna Daniel is a fiction writer at work on her first novel. She lives in Madison, Wisconsin, where she teaches creative writing and literature to undergraduate students. She is originally from Miami, Florida, and she has a B.A. from Columbia University and an M.F.A. from the University of Iowa Writers' Workshop.

Photo Credits

Cover © Jason Stemple; p. 2 Courtesy of Jane Yolen.

Design: Tahara Hasan; Editor: Annie Sommers